Common Car Sales Greeting Mistakes

What Drives Customers Away in the First Minute

Bruce Huddleston

Bedrock Heritage Publishing

Common Car Sales Greeting Mistakes

What Drives Customers Away in the First Minute

Copyright © 2026 by Bruce Huddleston

Author: Bruce Huddleston

Series: Car Sales Survival Guide Series — Book 9 of 10

Publisher: Bedrock Heritage Publishing

A Division of Life Guidance Consulting LLC — Tyler, Texas

ISBN: 978-1-972179-17-8 (Paperback)

ISBN: 978-1-972179-70-3 (EPUB)

Manufactured in the United States of America

Disclaimer

This book is based on the author's personal and professional experiences, observations, and opinions accumulated over a thirty-five-year career in the automotive industry. It is intended for educational and informational purposes only.

The stories and anecdotes contained in this book are drawn from real-world situations encountered throughout the author's career. However, names, identifying details, specific circumstances, employer names, dealership names, and individual characteristics have been changed, omitted, combined, or fictionalized to protect the privacy of the individuals involved. Any resemblance to specific living persons, current or former employers, or existing businesses is coincidental and unintentional.

No individual, dealership, organization, or employer referenced or implied in the stories within this book has reviewed, approved, or endorsed the content herein. The recollections and characterizations presented are solely the author's own perspective and memory of events and do not constitute a factual record, legal testimony, or statement of fact regarding any identifiable person or entity.

The sales strategies, techniques, and professional advice presented in this book reflect the author's personal approach and experience. Individual results will vary based on experience, effort, market conditions, dealership policies, and other factors beyond the author's control. Nothing in this book constitutes a guarantee of income, employment, or professional outcome.

The author and publisher have made reasonable efforts to ensure the accuracy of information presented at the time of writing. The author and publisher make no representations or warranties regarding the completeness, accuracy, or current applicability of the information contained herein, and expressly disclaim any liability arising from the use or application of the content of this book.

By reading this book, you acknowledge and agree that the author and publisher shall not be liable for any damages, losses, or claims arising directly or indirectly from the use of or reliance upon any information contained herein.

To every salesperson with the guts to look at what they're doing wrong. Anybody can read a book about what to do right. It takes a different kind of person to read a book about the mistakes they're probably making this week — and not get their back up about it. If you picked this one up, you're already that kind of person.

The salespeople who get good are the ones willing to look hard at the first minute and admit it could be better. This one's for them.

A Free Bonus For Readers

Your Complete Digital Script Library

Get the Car Sales Survival Quick-Reference Card — a free companion to this book that puts the key rules and techniques on one page you can keep at your desk.

Visit:

www.carsalessurvivalseries.com/scripts

Enter your email to claim your free reader bonus.
Print it. Keep it. Use it.

CONTENTS

Introduction

The First Minute Is Where Deals Die

You want to know where most deals die? Not in the numbers. Not in the finance office. Right at the door. In the first minute. Before you've said anything worth remembering.

I spent thirty-five years on the floor and in the management office, and I watched it happen more times than I can count. A customer pulls in ready to buy, and a salesperson kills the whole thing with a greeting. Not with a bad pitch. Not with a bad price. With a greeting. Sixty seconds, and it's over — the customer just hasn't told you yet.

Here's the part nobody wants to hear. The customer is grading you before you open your mouth. They watch how you come off the curb. They watch your face. They watch whether you saw the wife. By the time you stick your hand out, they've already decided how the next hour is going to feel. That decision is made mostly off the greeting, and it's made fast.

And here's the crueler part. You can't see yourself doing it. That's the whole problem with greeting mistakes — they don't feel like mistakes to the person making them. The guy who sprints to the door thinks he's being eager. The guy who leads with "What are you looking to buy today?" thinks he's being efficient. The guy who locks onto the husband and ignores the wife thinks he's focusing on the buyer. Every one of them is bleeding deals, and not one of them knows it.

This book is a catalog of those mistakes—one per chapter. I'm going to name them the way I name everything — the Pounce, the Hover, the canned open, the distracted hello — and for each one I'm going to put you on the other side of it, in the customer's shoes, so you can finally see what they see. Then I'm going to tell you what to do instead.

I'm not writing this from up on a hill. I made most of these mistakes myself when I was new, and I watched a hundred salespeople make the rest. None of this is theory. It's the stuff that quietly costs you deals while you're standing there thinking you did just fine.

So that's the question this whole book answers. What are you doing in the first minute that's costing you — and how do you stop? Let's go find out.

"The Rule: The customer decides in the first minute whether you've earned the next five. Win the minute, or you never get the five."

Chapter 1

The Pounce: Rushing the Customer at the Door

Some salespeople treat a car pulling in like a starting gun. The thing's barely stopped, and they're already moving — fast walk turning into a jog, talking before they arrive, crowding the door before the customer's even got a foot on the ground. That's the Pounce. And it kills more deals than any other greeting mistake I know.

I get why it happens. You're hungry. You want the up. Maybe somebody told you the early bird gets the deal, so you figure the faster you get there, the better. It feels like hustle. It feels like you're doing your job.

You're not. You're scaring people.

What the Customer Sees

Put yourself in the car. You drove down here half-nervous already, because everybody's got a story about a pushy car salesman. You pull in, you're getting your bearings, maybe your kid's still unbuckling in the back. And here comes a stranger at full speed, talking at you through the windshield before you've even opened the door. What does your gut do? It tightens. You go on defense. Before this person has said one useful thing, you've got your guard up and your exit planned. "We're just looking" is loaded and ready before they finish their sentence.

The Pounce reads as desperation. And desperation runs the wrong direction — it makes the customer nervous instead of comfortable. You wanted to look eager, and you looked needy. Those aren't the same thing, and the customer can tell the difference instantly.

FROM THE FLOOR

I was sitting in the front lobby of a dealership I managed — glass front wall, full view of the lot. A car pulled in. Two salespeople inside saw it at the same time. They both jumped up, ran for the door, and literally shoved each other trying to get through it first. Pushing and shoving like it was a race.

The customers, still in their car, watched every second of this.

The one who won was out of breath when he got there. He stuck his hand out and started talking before he'd even caught his breath, never looked at the wife, never acknowledged the kids in the back seat. Just started in.

The family looked around for a few minutes and left.

When I asked what happened, the salesperson said: "They were just looking."

No. They were watching. And what they watched told them everything they needed to know about what the next hour was going to feel like. The sprint didn't just cost a deal. It answered every one of the customer's silent questions about this place — and none of the answers were good.

That salesperson thought he won. He got to the door first. He beat the other guy. And he lost the family in under five minutes, then told me they were "just looking" — like the lot did it, not him.

How to Fix It

The fix is simple. Get there first if you can — being available matters. But get there calm. Walk at a normal pace. Let the customer get out of the car and stand up before you're on top of them. Give a small wave from a few steps off so they know you've seen them and you're coming, then close the distance like a human being, not a linebacker.

A relaxed approach tells the customer the next hour is going to be relaxed too. You don't have to choose between being available and being calm. Do both. Be the first one out there — and be the one who isn't out of breath when you arrive.

"The Rule: Be first if you can, but be calm no matter what. A greeting that feels like an ambush ends the deal at the door."

CROWDING THEM: NO ROOM TO BREATHE

THE POUNCE IS ABOUT speed. This one's about space. It's the mistake of the salesperson who finally learned not to sprint — so now he just stands too close and follows too soon. Same damage, slower fuse.

Crowding is standing a foot and a half from somebody you met four seconds ago. It's falling in behind a customer the second they step toward a car, so every time they turn around, there you are. It's never letting them get out, stretch their legs, and just look at the lot for a minute before you're in their bubble.

What the Customer Sees

A customer who just pulled in needs to orient. They want to see the lot, spot the car they came for, get their feet under them. That takes a few seconds of breathing room. When you crowd that, you take it away. Now they can't look at a vehicle without feeling watched. They can't say a quiet word to their spouse without you in earshot. They feel managed instead of helped — and a managed customer shuts down. They stop drifting toward what they actually want and start drifting toward the exit.

This is the opposite mistake from ignoring them, and salespeople who hear "don't ignore the customer" sometimes overcorrect straight into smothering. Both ends are wrong. Ignored, they feel like they don't matter. Crowded, they feel like they can't move. The customer wants to feel attended to and free at the same time. That's the needle you're threading.

How to Fix It

Give them room to land. Greet them, introduce yourself, let them know you're there — and then give them a little space to look. Hang back far enough that they can talk among themselves, close enough that the second they have a question, you're right there. Let them lead toward a car instead of herding them to one.

"Take your time, look around, I'll be right here when you've got a question" buys you more goodwill than hovering at their elbow ever will. Available, not on top of them. There's a world of difference, and the customer feels every inch of it.

"The Rule: Give them room to land. A customer who can breathe is a customer who'll talk."

CHAPTER 3

THE PRESSURE OPEN: "WHAT ARE YOU LOOKING TO BUY TODAY?"

THERE'S A QUESTION THAT ends conversations before they start. You've heard it. You've probably said it. "What are you looking to buy today?" Or some cousin of it — "You here to buy a car?" "What's your budget?" "You ready to make a deal today?" Anything that, in the first breath, announces I am here to sell you something.

Salespeople lead with it because it feels efficient. Cut to the chase. Qualify fast. Don't waste time. I understand the logic. The logic is wrong.

What the Customer Sees

Hear it from the customer's side. They walk up, still getting comfortable, and the very first thing out of your mouth is a buying question. What does that tell them? It tells them you don't care who they are — you care what they'll spend. You skipped right past hello and went straight to the wallet. Instantly, they harden. The walls go up. And the safest thing in the world for a cornered customer to say is "just looking." You handed them that line. You practically asked for it.

A buying question in the first breath turns a person into a transaction, and people don't like being a transaction. They walked in as somebody with a life and a reason for being there, and you reduced them to a sale before you knew their name.

FROM THE FLOOR

I walked into a well-known furniture store one afternoon looking for a recliner. Had a specific one in mind. Knew what I wanted to spend. Ready to buy. Three salespeople were sitting on a showroom couch. I could hear them — in earshot, not trying to be quiet — debating whose turn it was to help me. Like I was an interruption to whatever they had going on.

The one who drew the short straw walked over. No greeting. No name. No smile. Just: "What are you here to buy today?"

I said: "Nothing. I'm just looking. I'll let you know if I need help."

And I meant it. They'd lost me in the first five seconds. I didn't buy a thing there. Went somewhere else and bought the same recliner the same afternoon.

The irony is, I walked in ready to spend money. All they had to do was make me feel like a person instead of a chore. Instead, they spent more energy arguing over whose turn it was than they spent on the customer standing in front of them. That's not a sales problem. That's a culture problem. And it starts — and ends — with how a team treats the greeting.

I was the customer in that one. Ready to buy, money in hand, and they lost me in five seconds with one question and a bad attitude. I bought the exact same recliner somewhere else that afternoon. That's not a story about furniture. That's every car customer who ever walked off your lot because the first thing you did was reach for their wallet instead of their hand.

How to Fix It

Open like a person, not a salesman. Say hello. Give your name. Ask what brought them in today — not what they're buying, what brought them in. "Good afternoon, I'm Bruce — what brings you out today?" lands completely different than "What are you looking to buy?" One is curious about them. The other is hungry for them. The customer hears the difference immediately, every single time.

You'll get to the buying part. You'll get to budget, trade, and numbers, all of it. But not in the first breath. The first breath is for the human being. Earn the conversation before you ask for the sale.

"The Rule: Open like a person, not a salesman. Ask what brought them in — not what they're going to buy."

CHAPTER 4

TALKING TO ONE, IGNORING THE REST

A COUPLE WALKS UP. Maybe there's a kid or two. Maybe it's a guy and his buddy, or a daughter bringing her dad. You scan the group, decide in half a second who the buyer is, lock onto that person, and talk to them like the others aren't there. That's the mistake. And the person you ignored is very often the person who kills your deal.

I've watched a hundred salespeople do this. The husband and wife walk up, and the salesperson talks to the husband. Every question, every answer, every bit of eye contact — aimed at him. The wife might as well be a coat rack. The salesperson thinks he's being focused. He's being rude — and worse, he's being foolish, because he has no idea who actually makes the decision in that house.

What the Customer Sees

Be the ignored one for a second. You came to help pick a family car. You've got opinions, you've got concerns, maybe you're the one who handles the money. And this salesperson won't look at you. Won't ask you a thing. Treats you like you're just along for the ride. How do you feel about this guy? You don't trust him. You don't like him. And the whole drive home, you're the one saying "I didn't care for that salesman" — and the deal's dead in the driveway, and he never even knows why.

The person you wrote off is often the real decision-maker, the tiebreaker, or just the one whose bad feeling sinks the whole thing later. You don't get to pick who matters in that group. They all matter. Every set of eyes that walked up is part of this deal.

How to Fix It

Greet all of them. Make eye contact with each adult. Get down to the kid's level for a second and say hi — parents notice that, and they remember it. If it's a couple, address both, ask both, watch both. You'll figure out soon enough who's leaning which way, but you figure that out by including everyone, not by guessing at the door and betting the deal on it.

It costs you nothing to greet the whole party. It costs you everything to ignore the one who turned out to matter.

"The Rule: Greet every set of eyes that walked up. The one you ignore is the one who decides."

CHAPTER 5

THE CANNED, ROBOTIC GREETING

SOMEWHERE IN YOUR FIRST week, somebody handed you a greeting and told you to memorize it. "Welcome to the dealership, my name is Bruce, and you are?" Say it the same way every time. Smile here. Pause there. So you do — you run the script, word for word, with the same rhythm on the four hundredth customer that you used on the first.

The customer hears it. They always hear it.

There's a particular sound a memorized line makes. It's flat. It's a half-beat too smooth. The words are friendly, but the eyes are somewhere else, already three steps ahead to the next line. People are wired to catch this. We spend our whole lives reading whether somebody means what they're saying, and a recited greeting fails that test in about two seconds.

What the Customer Hears

When the greeting sounds canned, the customer stops listening to you and starts listening for the pitch. They know a script when they hear one, and a script tells them one thing: this isn't a conversation, it's a process, and I'm the next item in it. They've heard this exact voice from the guy at the other dealership, from the timeshare guy, from the cable company. The canned hello doesn't make you sound professional. It makes you sound like every salesperson they've ever wanted to get away from.

And here's what it costs you. A real greeting opens a door — the customer relaxes, talks back, tells you something true. A canned one closes it. You get the polite nod and the short answer because you signaled that this is a transaction, and they answered in kind.

I leaned on the script myself when I was green. It's a crutch, and I understand why — when you're nervous, the memorized line is something to hold onto. But the crutch is the problem. You get so busy delivering the words right that you forget there's a person standing in front of you.

How to Fix It

Throw out the recital. Keep the structure. There's nothing wrong with knowing you'll say hello, give your name, and ask an opening question — that's just sense. What kills it is delivering it like a recording. Look the person in the eye. Say it the way you'd say it to somebody you actually wanted to meet. Let it come out a little different every time, because every customer is a little different.

"Hey, afternoon — I'm Bruce. What's got you out today?" said like a human being beats the prettiest memorized speech ever written. The customer isn't grading your wording. They're reading whether you're real. Be real, and the words take care of themselves.

"The Rule: A real hello beats a perfect one. Say it like you mean it, or don't bother saying it at all."

Chapter 6

The Distracted Greeting

THIS ONE'S QUIETER THAN the Pounce, but it does just as much damage. The distracted greeting. You walk up to the customer and say all the right words — but your phone's in your hand, or you're tossing one last comment over your shoulder to a buddy, or your eyes keep flicking past the customer to the better-looking up that just pulled in behind them.

You think you're multitasking. The customer thinks you don't care.

What the Customer Feels

Attention is the one thing a customer can feel instantly, and the absence of it even faster. When your eyes are on your phone during the hello, the customer doesn't hear "welcome" — they hear "you're an interruption." When you finish a laugh with a coworker before you turn to them, they file it away: I'm second to whatever that was. When you scan over their shoulder for a fresh up, they catch it — every time — because people always know when they've lost your eyes.

And it's insulting in a way the customer won't say out loud. They drove down, they walked up, they're standing right in front of you — and you can't give them the one thing that costs you nothing. Full attention is the cheapest gift in sales and somehow the rarest. The customer who feels half-greeted doesn't argue about it. They just decide you're not worth their afternoon, and they drift.

How to Fix It

Put the phone away before you walk out. Not in your pocket where you'll sneak a look — away. End the coworker conversation before you start the customer one; the coworker can wait, the customer can't. And when somebody's in front of you, they get all of you. Eyes on them. Body turned to them. Whatever's happening on the rest of the lot will still be there in ninety seconds.

The fix here is almost embarrassingly simple, which is exactly why so few people do it. Just be all the way there. For the length of a greeting, the person in front of you is the only person on the lot. Give them that, and you're already ahead of most of the floor.

"The Rule: Whoever's in front of you gets all of you. A half-greeting tells the customer they're half-important."

Chapter 7

Prejudging the Up

A CAR PULLS IN. Before the customer's even out of it, you've done the math. Old trade-in. Work clothes. Kid's car seat in the back. You've decided — this one's a tire-kicker, a payment shopper, a be-back at best. And without meaning to, you greet them like it. A little less energy. A little less interest. Already halfway to the next up in your head.

That's prejudging the up, and it's one of the most expensive habits on the lot — because you're wrong more than you think, and the customer can feel exactly what you decided about them.

What the Customer Feels

Here's the thing nobody tells you: people know when they've been written off. They can't always name it, but they feel it. The handshake that's a little limp. The eyes that don't quite land. The energy that says you're not really worth my time. A customer who walks up excited and gets a lukewarm greeting because you decided they couldn't afford it — that customer deflates, then leaves, then buys from the salesperson down the road who treated them like a buyer.

Because that's how it actually goes. The guy in the paint-stained work shirt owns the contracting company. The couple in the beat-up trade just sold a house. The quiet one who "looks like a be-back" has cash and came in to spend it today. I've seen every one of these, more than once. The customer you wrote off in the parking lot is constantly the one who buys — just not from you.

I did this myself, early on, and got humbled hard enough times that I quit. You cannot tell who's going to buy by looking at the car they drove up in or the shoes they've got on. You just can't. Anybody who tells you they can is bragging about the deals they lost.

How to Fix It

Greet every up like they're the best customer of your day — because one of them is, and you don't get to know which one in advance. Same energy, same eye contact, same respect, every car, every time. Treat the work boots and the luxury sedan exactly alike at the door.

It isn't just the right thing to do, though it is that. It's the smart thing. The salesperson who greets everybody like a real buyer catches the deals everybody else prejudged away. Let the other guys sort customers by their shoes. You'll be cashing the commissions they threw out.

"The Rule: You can't tell who'll buy by what they drove up in. Greet every up like the best one of the day."

The Hover: Stalking the Lot

You greeted them right. You gave them a little space, the way Chapter 2 said to. So far so good. And then you ruined it by following them around the lot at ten paces like a shadow they can't shake.

That's the Hover. Never close enough to actually help, never far enough to let them breathe. Every time the customer turns around — there you are. They step behind a truck to say a word to their spouse, and somehow you've drifted to the end of that same row. You think you're being attentive. You're being creepy.

What the Customer Feels

There's a specific discomfort to being followed, and customers feel it on a car lot the same way they'd feel it walking through a parking garage at night. They can't relax. They can't have a real conversation with the person they came with, because you're always within earshot. They can't look at a car honestly, because they know the second they show interest, you'll pounce. So they do the only thing they can: cut the visit short and get out from under your shadow.

The cruel part is that the Hover comes from a good instinct — you don't want to abandon them, you want to be there when they need you. But there's a canyon between available and lurking, and the customer knows exactly which side of it you're on. Available feels like help. Hovering feels like being watched.

How to Fix It

Give them a reason to come back to you, then actually back off. "Take your time — I'll be right over by the office, just wave when you've got a question." Then go stand by the office. Find a little something to do so you're not just staring at them. Let them look in peace. When they wave, or when you see them lingering on one car — circling it, opening the door — that's your cue, and now you walk over welcome instead of resented.

Being available means they know where you are and that you're easy to reach. It does not mean you're three steps behind them everywhere they go. Plant yourself, stay visible, let them come to you. The customer who isn't being stalked is the customer who relaxes enough to actually buy.

"The Rule: Be easy to find, not impossible to lose. Hovering feels like being watched, not helped."

CHAPTER 8

THE FRANTIC APPROACH: LETTING THEM SEE YOU SWEAT

BACK IN CHAPTER 1, we talked about the Pounce — moving too fast at the customer. This is its close cousin, and it's about something a little different. Not your speed. Your state. The frantic approach is arriving rushed, breathless, scattered — papers half in your hand, words tumbling out, energy bouncing all over the place. You might not have even sprinted. You can be frantic standing still.

And the customer reads your state before they read your words. If you show up wound up, they wind up too.

What the Customer Sees

Calm is contagious. So is panic. When you walk up flustered — patting your pockets for a pen, talking too fast, sweat on your forehead, eyes a little wild — the customer's body does the math instantly: if this is how the hello goes, what's the next two hours going to be like? They picture the test drive, the numbers, the finance office, all of it running at this same frantic pitch, and they decide they don't want any part of it. Not because you're a bad person. Because you made buying a car look stressful, and they walked in stressed enough already.

Customers want to feel like they're in steady hands. A frantic greeting tells them they're not. It says you're barely holding it together — and nobody wants to hand fifteen or thirty thousand dollars to somebody who's barely holding it together.

FROM THE FLOOR

The summer heat in Texas is no joke. I was managing a used car lot — no air conditioning on the lot, obviously — and it was one of those July afternoons where the asphalt is soft, and the air feels like a wet towel. A couple pulled in. I watched my newest salesperson sprint out to meet them — which was already the wrong move — and by the time he got to them, he was visibly sweating through his shirt. The customers looked at him, looked at each other, and said they were just looking. He came back inside looking defeated.

I went out. Introduced myself. Said: "Sorry about the heat — let me know if you want to step inside and cool off while we talk." That's all it took. They came inside. We sold them a car in ninety minutes. The first salesperson did everything wrong before he said a word. I did one thing right: I acknowledged where they were before I asked anything of them.

Notice what actually won that deal. It wasn't a pitch. It wasn't a price. It was composure and one sentence that acknowledged where the customer was before asking anything of them. The new guy lost them by showing up frantic. I got them back by showing up calm: same customers, same lot, same brutal heat. The only thing that changed was the temperature of the salesperson.

How to Fix It

Slow your approach down on purpose. If you've been moving fast, stop for one second before you reach them and take a breath. Let your shoulders drop. Walk the last few steps at an easy pace. Have your pen already on you so you're not fishing for it. And if conditions are rough — heat, rain, whatever — name it and offer relief instead of pretending it isn't happening: "Brutal out here, isn't it? Step inside where it's cool and we'll talk."

You set the temperature of the whole interaction in the first ten seconds. If you're calm, they get calm. If you're scattered, they get nervous, and then they get gone. Composure isn't a personality trait you're either born with or not. It's a choice you make in the approach, every single time. Make it.

"The Rule: You set the temperature in the first ten seconds. Show up calm — the customer catches whatever you're carrying."

CHAPTER 9

BAD SIGNALS: THE BODY THAT PUSHES PEOPLE AWAY

EVERYTHING WE'VE COVERED SO far has been about what you do and what you say. This chapter is about what you're saying before you say anything. Because the customer starts reading you the second you come into view, and your body is broadcasting the whole time — whether you mean it to or not.

I'm not going to give you a full body language seminar here. I just want to name the silent signals that quietly kill a greeting before your first word lands, because most salespeople have no idea they're sending them.

The Signals That Push People Away

No eye contact. You greet the customer while looking at the car, the lot, the ground — anywhere but their eyes. To them, that reads as shifty or uninterested, and trust never gets off the ground.

No smile. A flat, blank face on the approach tells the customer you'd rather be anywhere else. They mirror it right back, and now you're both stiff before a word's been said.

Slumped posture, dragging energy. Shoulders rounded, feet shuffling, like the up is a chore. The customer sees somebody who doesn't want to be there, and decides they don't either.

Arms crossed. It reads as closed off — bored, even hostile. You might just be cold, or you might stand that way out of habit. Doesn't matter. The customer reads a wall.

The handshake. Two ways to blow it. The limp one — the dead-fish hand that says no confidence, no presence. And the crusher — the guy who turns it into a contest and leaves the customer's knuckles aching. Both leave a bad taste in the first three seconds.

What the Customer Feels

Here's the trouble with all of these: they happen before you've earned any benefit of the doubt. Later in the conversation, a customer might forgive a flat moment because they've already decided they like you. But in the first minute, you're all signal and no track record. The crossed arms and the dead-fish handshake are the only data they've got, so they weigh heavy. You can talk like a champion thirty seconds later — but if your body opened with the wrong message, you're already digging out of a hole.

How to Fix It

You don't need to overthink this, and you definitely don't need to fake it. Walk up like you're glad to see them — because if you love this business, you should be. Look them in the eye. Let a real smile happen. Stand up straight, arms loose and open at your sides. Offer a handshake that's firm and warm and over in a second — no contest, no limp.

None of that is acting. It's just letting your body say the same friendly thing your mouth is about to. When the signals and the words agree, the customer believes you. When they fight each other, the customer believes the body every time.

"The Rule: Your body greets the customer before your mouth does. Make sure it's saying the same friendly thing."

Chapter 10

Pitching Before You Listen

Some salespeople treat the greeting like the opening of a commercial. The customer's barely said hello, and they're off — rattling features, this month's specials, the rebate, the low APR, the model that just came in. All of it aimed at a person they know nothing about. That's pitching before you listen, and it's the greeting that's all about the salesperson.

The intention's usually good. You want to be helpful, you want to show you know your stuff. But you're transmitting when you should be receiving, and you're answering questions the customer never asked.

What the Customer Feels

Picture walking into a store, and the second you're through the door, somebody starts reading you the catalog. You haven't told them what you came for. You haven't said a word about your situation. And they're already three deep into a pitch for something you may not want at all. How long before you're looking for the exit?

That's the car customer getting the feature dump. They came in with a reason — a growing family, a long commute, a trade they're upside down on, a teenager who just got a license. Every bit of that matters, and you can't learn any of it while you're the one talking. The pitch-first greeting tells the customer you don't care what they need; you care what you're selling. And it wastes the time of both of you, because half of what you're pitching has nothing to do with why they came.

There's another cost. When you pitch first, you give the customer nothing to do but resist. You've made it a presentation, and the only move they've got left is to push back or tune out. When you ask first, you give them something to do — talk about themselves, which people are glad to do. One opens them up. The other shuts them down.

How to Fix It

Flip it. Your first job in the greeting isn't to transmit — it's to find out. Ask, then shut up and actually listen. "What's got you looking today?" "What are you driving now?" "What's working or not working about it?" Then let them answer without jumping in to pitch the second they pause for breath.

Everything you learn in those first thirty seconds of listening makes every word you say afterward land ten times harder, because now you're talking about their situation instead of your inventory. The feature that means nothing to one customer is the whole deal for the next — and the only way to know which is which is to listen first. Sell less in the greeting. Learn more. The selling gets easy once you know who you're selling to.

"The Rule: The first job of the greeting is to listen, not to pitch. You can't sell to somebody you haven't heard."

CHAPTER II

FORGETTING WHAT THE GREETING IS FOR

HERE'S A MISTAKE THAT hides underneath all the others, because it isn't about what you do in the greeting — it's about what you think the greeting is. A lot of salespeople walk up to a customer, believing the greeting is where you win the deal. So they load it up. They try to build rapport and qualify the buyer and pitch the hot unit and lock down a test drive, all inside the first sixty seconds. And it falls apart, because they're asking the greeting to do a job it was never meant to do.

The greeting is not a close. It's an opening. That's the whole thing.

What the Greeting Is Actually For

Let me say it plain. The goal of the greeting is not to sell a car. The goal of the greeting is to earn the next five minutes. That's it. You're not trying to get to "yes" at the door. You're trying to get to a real conversation — one where the customer is comfortable, talking, willing to tell you what they're after. Win that, and the car practically sells itself later. Skip it, and there is no later.

When you forget this, you push too hard, too soon. You're closing before you've opened. The customer feels the weight of it — they can tell you're trying to wrap something up before it's even started, and it makes them want to slow down or back out. You went for the whole deal in the first minute, and in reaching for everything, you knocked over the one thing that was actually on the table: the start of a conversation.

The Fumbled Hand-Off

There's a flip side, too. Some salespeople nail the hello — warm, calm, all of it — and then just stall. They greeted the customer fine and have no idea what comes next. The conversation dies in an awkward silence, or they panic and lurch into a pitch. They treated the greeting as the finish line instead of the doorway, so once they got through it, they didn't know where to go.

A good greeting hands off smoothly into a real conversation. "What's got you out today?" leads to an answer, the answer leads to a question, and now you're talking. The greeting's job is done the moment the conversation is breathing on its own. Knowing that takes the pressure off — you don't have to accomplish everything at the door. You just have to open it and walk through.

How to Fix It

Right-size the greeting. Ask it to do one job: earn the next five minutes. Say hello like a human, give your name, ask what brought them in, and listen to the answer like it's the most interesting thing you'll hear all day. Then follow it into a conversation. Don't pitch, don't qualify hard, don't close. Just open, and keep it open.

The salespeople who understand this seem relaxed at the door, because they are. They're not carrying the whole deal on the first sentence. They know the greeting is one move — the first one — and they're content to make it well and let the rest follow.

"The Rule: The greeting isn't the close. Its only job is to earn the next five minutes — so let it."

Chapter 12

Getting It Right: The Greeting That Makes Them Stay

We've spent twelve chapters on what not to do. Let's finish with what right looks like — because here's the good news buried in this whole book: the greeting done right isn't some advanced technique you have to master. It's just the absence of all the mistakes we've named. Take away the Pounce, the crowding, the pressure open, the prejudging, the hover, the frantic energy, the bad signals, the pitch-first reflex — and what's left is a clean, simple, professional greeting. That's it. You don't add anything fancy. You just stop doing the things that drive people off.

What It Looks Like

Picture it. A car pulls in. You don't sprint — you stand, and you head out at an easy pace, a small wave to let them know you've seen them. You let them get out and get their bearings. You walk up calm, glad to see them, look them in the eye, real smile, easy handshake. You greet everybody who came, not just the one you guessed was the buyer. You say hello like a person, not a recording. "Afternoon — I'm Bruce. What's got you out today?"

Then you listen. You don't pitch. You don't qualify them like a loan officer. You let them tell you why they're there, and you follow their lead — fast if they're ready to move fast, slow if they need to wander. You give them room without disappearing. You stay easy to find. And just like that, the deal's first minute is behind you, and a real conversation is underway. No pressure. No mistakes. Just an opening done well.

FROM THE FLOOR

One afternoon, a customer pulled into the lot in a taxi. That caught my attention — most people drive themselves in. This one stepped out and walked directly toward a specific vehicle, like he already knew exactly what he was looking for.

I didn't rush. I stood up, walked out at a normal pace, gave him a small wave as I crossed the lot. When I reached him, I introduced myself and told him I'd be glad to help if he had any questions.

He told me he'd just gotten off a flight and came straight from the airport. His vehicle had been destroyed in a fire in the parking lot while he was traveling. He'd seen one of our ads and came directly to us. He knew which vehicle he wanted. He just needed to drive it and confirm it.

We took a short test drive. Came back. He asked how to make out the check.

Start to finish, maybe forty-five minutes. The deal was easy because the approach was right. No pressure, no assumptions, no rushing. Just a professional greeting and a willingness to follow the customer's lead.

Not every customer comes in that ready to buy. But every customer deserves that same professional opening. You never know which one is going to be the taxi customer — the one who's already decided and just needs someone to not get in their way.

Forty-five minutes, start to finish, and the reason was the approach. He'd already decided — all I had to do was not get in his way. That's the lesson hiding in this whole book. Most customers aren't looking for a great salesperson. They're looking for one who won't mess it up. Get the greeting right, and you clear the path. Get it wrong, and you're the obstacle.

Make It Your Default

Here's what I want you to take off this lot. The right greeting isn't a performance you switch on for the promising-looking ups. It's your default — the same calm, warm, attentive opening for every car, every customer, every time. The taxi customer who's ready to write a check today and the tire-kicker who might be a buyer next month both get the same professional hello. Because you can't tell them apart at the door, and because it's just who you are now.

You've got the catalog of mistakes. You know what they look like and what they cost. Now you know what's left when you strip them away — and it isn't complicated, it isn't a gimmick, and it works. Go greet your next up like you mean it.

"The Rule: Getting it right is just the mistakes removed. Greet every up calm, warm, and attentive — and get out of the buyer's way."

CONCLUSION

Let me leave you with the simplest version of everything in this book. The first minute decides more than it has any right to. The customer renders a verdict off your greeting — fast, mostly silent, and largely set before you've said anything that matters. Lose that minute, and most of the time you never even find out you lost it. They just say "I'm just looking," and they're gone.

Almost every mistake in these pages comes from the same root: forgetting there's a real person on the other end, with their own nerves and reasons and a pretty good radar for salespeople. The Pounce, the pressure open, the prejudging, the hover, the feature dump — every one of them is a way of treating the customer like a transaction instead of a human being. And every one of them is invisible to the person doing it. That's why this book exists. Not because you're careless, but because you can't see your own greeting from the customer's side. Now you can.

The fixes aren't hard. They're not even really techniques. Slow down. Stay calm. Greet everybody. Be real. Pay attention. Don't judge. Don't smother. Listen before you pitch. Remember, the greeting is an opening, not a close. None of that requires talent. It requires awareness and the willingness to look honestly at what you're doing in the first minute.

I made most of these mistakes myself. I watched good people make the rest, lose deals they should have had, and never understand why. You don't have to be one of them. You've got the whole catalog now — what drives customers away, what it costs, and what to do instead. The next part is up to you. Walk out there tomorrow and get the first minute right. The rest of the deal gets a whole lot easier when you do.

Tips for the Sales Manager

This part's for the managers. If you run a floor, the greeting isn't just your salespeople's problem — it's yours, because the first minute on your lot is happening dozens of times a day, whether you're watching it or not, and it's quietly making or costing you deals across the whole team.

Here's the first thing to understand: most of the mistakes in this book don't come from bad attitudes. They come from people who can't see themselves. Your salesperson sprinting to the door thinks he's hustling. Your guy who prejudges the work truck up thinks he's reading the room. They're not being lazy or careless. They're blind to their own greeting, same as everybody is. Which means you can't fix it by chewing them out. You fix it by showing them what you see.

So go watch. Stand where you can see the lot and just observe the greetings — the approach, the pace, the eyes, whether they greet the whole party, what they lead with. You'll spot the patterns fast. Then coach the behavior, not the person. "I watched you go out to that couple — you got there a little hot, take a breath on the walk out next time" lands. "Quit being so desperate" does not. Name the mistake, point at the fix, keep it about the next up instead of the last one.

Build it into the culture, too. When the whole team knows the greeting matters — that nobody argues over whose turn it is while a customer stands there, that everybody gets greeted calm and welcomed regardless of what they drove up in — the customer experience gets consistent instead of depending on which salesperson happened to catch the up. That consistency is worth real money over a month.

And don't forget the new people. The greeting is where they're most nervous and most likely to freeze, hesitate, or overcompensate into a Pounce. A manager who encourages them — who tells them what they did right, not just what they blew — builds their confidence faster than any amount of correction. The salesperson who feels supported takes the next up instead of dreading it.

You set the standard for the first minute. Your team greets the way you teach them to, and the way you tolerate. Make the greeting a priority out loud, coach it on the floor, and you'll see it in the numbers.

APPENDIX

The Rules

Every chapter in this book ends with one rule — the single thing most worth remembering. Here they all are in one place. Read them before your shift. Read them after a slow day. They're the whole book boiled down to fourteen lines.

Introduction

The Rule: The customer decides in the first minute whether you've earned the next five. Win the minute, or you never get the five.

Chapter 1 — The Pounce

"The Rule: Be first if you can, but be calm no matter what. A greeting that feels like an ambush ends the deal at the door."

Chapter 2 — Crowding Them

"The Rule: Give them room to land. A customer who can breathe is a customer who'll talk."

Chapter 3 — The Pressure Open

"The Rule: Open like a person, not a salesman. Ask what brought them in — not what they're going to buy."

Chapter 4 — Talking to One, Ignoring the Rest

"The Rule: Greet every set of eyes that walked up. The one you ignore is the one who decides."

Chapter 5 — The Canned, Robotic Greeting

"The Rule: A real hello beats a perfect one. Say it like you mean it, or don't bother saying it at all."

Chapter 6 — The Distracted Greeting

"The Rule: Whoever's in front of you gets all of you. A half-greeting tells the customer they're half-important."

Chapter 7 — Prejudging the Up

"The Rule: You can't tell who'll buy by what they drove up in. Greet every up like the best one of the day."

Chapter 8 — The Hover

"The Rule: Be easy to find, not impossible to lose. Hovering feels like being watched, not helped."

Chapter 9 — The Frantic Approach

"The Rule: You set the temperature in the first ten seconds. Show up calm — the customer catches whatever you're carrying."

Chapter 10 — Bad Signals

"The Rule: Your body greets the customer before your mouth does. Make sure it's saying the same friendly thing."

Chapter 11 — Pitching Before You Listen

"The Rule: The first job of the greeting is to listen, not to pitch. You can't sell to somebody you haven't heard."

Chapter 12 — Forgetting What the Greeting Is For

"The Rule: The greeting isn't the close. Its only job is to earn the next five minutes — so let it."

Chapter 13 — Getting It Right

"The Rule: Getting it right is just the mistakes removed. Greet every up calm, warm, and attentive — and get out of the buyer's way."

Also Available

FLAGSHIP

The Complete Car Sales Survival Guide

The No-BS Playbook for New Automotive Salespeople

Book 1 — The Meet and Greet Playbook

How to Make Powerful First Impressions with Customers, Clients, and Guests

Book 2 — The First 60 Seconds in Car Sales

A Proven Meet and Greet System to Build Trust and Start More Conversations

Book 3 — How to Handle "I'm Just Looking" in Car Sales

A Simple System to Turn Brush-Offs into Productive Conversations

Book 4 — Body Language in Car Sales

How Posture, Eye Contact, and Presence Build Customer Trust

Book 5 — Greeting Customers on the Lot

How to Approach Buyers Without Pressure

Book 6 — The Ten-Second Rule in Car Sales

Why First Impressions Determine Whether Customers Stay or Leave

Book 7 — The Car Sales Conversation Starter Guide

How to Begin Natural Conversations That Lead to Sales

Book 8 — Car Sales Confidence for New Salespeople

How to Approach Customers Without Fear or Hesitation

Book 9 — Common Car Sales Greeting Mistakes

What Drives Customers Away in the First Minute

Book 10 — The First Five Minutes With a Car Buyer

How to Transition from Greeting to Conversation and Move Toward the Sale

WORK WITH BRUCE

If you're interested in one-on-one coaching, sales team training, or dealership consulting, Bruce works with individuals and organizations through Life Guidance Consulting.

For inquiries:

www.lifeguidanceconsulting.com

bruce@lifeguidanceconsulting.com

For publishing inquiries or bulk orders:

www.bedrockheritagepublishing.com

info@bedrockheritagepublishing.com

About the Author

Bruce Huddleston spent thirty-five years in the automotive industry, working every level of the business from showroom floor salesperson to finance manager, sales manager, used car manager, and general manager. His career included new-car franchise dealerships, independent used-car operations, and a decade in buy-here, pay-here — giving him a breadth of experience that few in the industry can match.

He began as a high school dropout who needed a job and ended up discovering a profession. He ended as a veteran who had trained hundreds of salespeople, managed multiple departments, and built a reputation for straight talk in an industry that doesn't always reward it.

Since retiring, Bruce has opened a life coaching practice, assists his wife with her mental health therapy practice, and operates Bedrock Heritage Publishing, a division of Life Guidance Consulting LLC, where he writes practical guides for sales professionals across multiple industries.

The Complete Car Sales Survival Guide is his flagship work. The Car Sales Survival Guide Series — a collection of focused training guides on specific sales skills — is built on the same foundation of real experience, honest insight, and zero tolerance for the kind of nonsense that gives sales a bad name.

He lives in Tyler, Texas.

A Quick Favor

If *Common Car Sales Greeting Mistakes* helped you — if it changed how you walk onto a lot, how you read a customer, or how you think about what your body is saying before you open your mouth — I'd be grateful if you'd take two minutes to leave a review wherever you bought it.

Reviews matter more than most people realize. They help other salespeople find books that can actually make a difference in their work. And honest feedback helps me keep writing things worth reading.

You can simply scan the QR code below.

https://www.amazon.com/review/create-review/?asin=1972179179

www.bedrockheritagepublishing.com

Thank you for spending time with this book. Now go to work.

— Bruce Huddleston